BENEATH
—THE—
GAZA SKY

SHADI SALEM

Fomite
Burlington, VT

ISBN-13: 978-1-967022-01-4
Library of Congress Control Number: 2025934205
Fomite
58 Peru Street
Burlington, VT 05401
www.fomitepress.com
01-15-2026

Dedication

To my dear parents, my father, from whom I learned patience and perseverance, and my mother, the embodiment of tenderness and unconditional love, who carried me in her heart and soul, always standing by my side with unwavering support and boundless encouragement.

To my beloved wife, my refuge in both presence and absence, whose strength and love grant me resilience; to my son Mohammed and my daughter Massa, the heartbeat of my soul and the light of my life, you are my eternal promise. No matter how far life takes us apart, my heart will always find its way back to you.

To my brothers and sisters, my lifelong companions in pain and hope, and to my dear friends in Gaza, who share with me both joy and sorrow, together, we will remain strong and face all challenges with unwavering determination.

To every martyr, wounded soul, and prisoner; to all who have sacrificed and endured suffering, this work is dedicated to honoring your noble sacrifices and the purity of your spirit. And to every patient and resilient soul in my homeland, where injustice and suffering persist, yet faith and resilience remain unshaken against adversity.

1. Gaza

The pen calls for attention, yet this tale isn't just any tale, for the tale is of Gaza. I can't grasp the pen with my delicate fingers, for sometimes the pen transforms into a sharp knife that wounds the paper of the soul. I can't write and fly away at the same time, nor can I abandon the pen to rest.

Gaza: the city of light that has never seen light before, yet remains the source of light, the city of peace that has never seen peace. Gaza, the fragrance emanating from the fragments and tears of wounds, Gaza, the body exhausted by wars, Gaza, betrayed by near and far with their silent conspiracies, leaving her to bleed alone. Gaza, the beautiful small girl, 25 miles long, and a width ranging between 4 and 7 miles, with a total area of 141 square miles. Approximately 2 million Palestinians grow within her, in the heart of this captivating girl, all dreaming of return no matter how long it takes.

Gaza's beautiful port

Gaza, a land brimming with tales of resilience and hope, may be small in size, but it is vast in spirit and strength. I live in a small city located in the northernmost part of Gaza, where only a 10-minute walk separates us from the Israeli-occupier fence. In this place, young people carry the torch of hope and gather to organize a hiking trip towards the southernmost point, to the Rafah crossing, covering this distance on foot in six hours, while the same journey takes about 45 minutes by car.

The wonderful Abu Hasira Roundabout

When we head from east to west, we find the sea, which is the only outlet for the people of Gaza. The walk to the sea takes about fifty minutes; it can be reached by car in just fifteen. These short distances highlight how small Gaza's area is, yet at the same time, they reveal the determination and perseverance of its people.

In Gaza, we see men and young boys standing firm against challenges, courageous women providing support and sacrifices, and elders carrying the wisdom and patience of the ages in their hearts. This small city shows us that greatness is not measured by size, but by determination and will. In Gaza, the meanings of resilience and challenge are evident in every corner, painting a picture of unbreakable hope and strength.

We are besieged on all side, as if we live in a large open prison. Imagine that I cannot visit the other part of my people in the West Bank, even

6

though the distance between us is no more than an hour by car. Due to the occupation's restrictions, we, the youth, are prohibited from visiting that land, an inseparable part of our homeland. Al-Aqsa Mosque, the first Qibla for Muslims and one of the most sacred places, remains out of our reach despite its geographical proximity.

I remember the moment I was accepted into a university in the United States. I was thrilled at the opportunity to achieve my dreams, but my joy quickly faded when I remembered that there is no embassy or consular office in the Gaza Strip. I had to schedule an appointment for the interview at the American embassy in Jerusalem. It was not easy; I faced many difficulties in getting there. However, the most frustrating part was when my application was rejected twice due to so-called security bans. This is the answer for everyone; we live in a closed circle of deprivation and frustration.

Gaza is considered one of the oldest known cities in history. Its definitive naming remains uncertain, as these names have changed and distorted with the civilizations that struggled over it. Among the Canaanites, it was known as "Hazuati," while the Egyptians called it "Ghazatu." The Assyrians and Greeks named it "Azati" and "Fasus," respectively. The Hebrews called it "Aza," and the Crusaders named it "Ghazzah." The Turks retained its Arabic name "Gaza," while the English called it "Gaza."

Historians, as is usual with many ancient cities, are divided regarding the reason for naming Gaza. Some suggest it derives from "military strength," while others propose it means "wealth." Still others view it as "distinct" or "special," pointing to significant qualities that distinguish it from other cities.

The Arabs had a close connection with Gaza. Their traders visited it in commercial ventures and journeys, considering it an important center for several trade routes. It was one of the destinations of the famous journeys mentioned in the Quran in Surah Quraish, known as "the winter and summer journeys." The Quraysh tribe traveled to Yemen in winter and to Gaza and the outskirts of Syria in summer. It was during one of these summer journeys that Hashim bin Abd Manaf, the Prophet Muhammad's (peace be upon him) great-grandfather, died and was buried in Gaza in the mosque in the Daraj neighborhood, now known as Hashim Mosque.

Gaza was formerly part of the Ottoman Empire before coming under British occupation from 1918 to 1948. From 1948 to 1967, it was under Egyptian control. In 1993, under the Oslo Accords, Israel granted limited self-rule to the Palestinian Authority in Gaza. Since 2007, the Gaza Strip has effectively been ruled as a single-party state by the Hamas move-

Shadi with his grandmother, Khadra

ment.

I loved sitting with my grandmother, the wise woman who had lived through all the wars that affected Palestine and knew many details about our ancestors. I enjoyed listening to her stories and some of the older family members, and learning things I wouldn't have known.

My grandmother told me about my first grandfather, who initially married one of his relatives, but fate did not allow them to have children. He then married a second time, but the issue of having children persisted, so he decided not to marry again. When my grandfather turned fifty-three, a strange story unfolded: My grandfather's father had married one of his relatives, but their marriage ended in divorce. She then married another man and had a duaghter with him. After her second husband passed away, problems arose with her late husband's family, so she wanted to marry her daughter to one of her relatives to ensure her protection. My grandfather married this woman and had three sons with her: Musa, Ahmed, and Mohammed, and a daughter named Jamila.

One day, I asked my grandmother about Gaza, and she wisely replied, "My dear, Gaza is unconquerable." She used to say this phrase to emphasize Gaza's strength and resilience against its enemies. The occupier

Palestinian fighters

knew well that anyone who tried to conquer Gaza would inevitably lose, which is why they could never fully impose their control over it.

My grandmother was an endless source of inspiration and knowledge for me. Her stories painted a clear picture of our ancestors and their lives, teaching me that true strength does not come from numbers or weapons, but from believing in justice, holding on to it, and standing firm against oppression. For her, Gaza was a symbol of this strength, a city small in area, but great in spirit and in its people. In my writings, my grandmother's memories and words will always remain alive, carrying a message of hope and resilience for future generations.

Gaza, this small spot, is cherished by all who inhabit or visit it. Between its fertile land and its blue sea, hope and aspirations for a better future emerge. Every day is a new opportunity to build dreams and achieve accomplishments. Despite the pain, it finds joy, wealth amidst poverty, love amidst war, goodness amidst evil, will amidst challenges, courage amidst weakness. Gaza is a land of perseverance and resilience, defying hardships with its strong spirit and firm determination. In every corner, life pulsates and shines with its diverse colors, a unique blend of heritage, culture, and sacrifice. In its streets, voices and colors converge, scents and flavors blend, creating an artistic tableau reflecting the beauty of life despite adversity. Here, people exchange laughter and tears, and the spirit of giving and solidarity manifests in every situation.

In Gaza, families and friends gather around food tables to share stories and laughter, spreading joy and happiness among people despite the difficult circumstances they face. Gaza is not only renowned for its resilience and the beauty of its shores, but also for its delicious cuisine and traditional dishes that reflect its rich, diverse heritage. Authentic Palestinian flavors are showcased in dishes like maqluba, muftool, musakhan, mansaf, and stuffed grape leaves, which are symbols of the Palestinian people's history and culture.

In Gaza, you will find many unique, beautiful restaurants, with many of them boasting views of the Gaza Sea. The amusing part is that some of these restaurants have international names but do not serve the corresponding cuisine. For example, the Thai restaurant serves nothing related to Thai food, the Italian restaurant has no Italian dishes, and there is even a Turkish restaurant that offers everything but Turkish food. These peculiarities add a distinctive character to the dining experience in Gaza, making it an unforgettable part of a visit to this resilient city.

One of my Malaysian friends, who lives near Thailand, heard about the Thai restaurant in Gaza and wanted to visit it to try some Thai dishes. When he went there, he was astonished and said, "This restaurant has not even a hint of Thai food." This amusing experience became an another memorable story about Gaza and its restaurants.

Sunset over Gaza City

2. Beneath the Gaza Sky

In 1992, I emerged under the sky of Gaza, and grew up in a modest family. My father had to leave school during his middle school years to work and support his siblings and father, while my mother also left school during her middle school years due to the family's circumstances. During that time, it was common for many people to leave school due to various reasons.

I remember, even as a child, I loved asking my parents, especially my mother, about the past. I was particularly curious about my mother's childhood, especially since she gave birth to twins in her first pregnancy. I asked her about the reason for naming me Shadi and my brother Fadi. She said she was very scared because it was her first pregnancy, and she was thin, so people doubted whether she was carrying twins. She never thought about names and prayed for God to help her and stand by her during her pregnancy until delivery. The day she had been waiting for finally came, to relieve her from the worries that almost killed her during the pregnancy. Mom says, "There was a midwife present during the delivery, and during the conversation with my husband, I suggested we prepare two cribs for the babies. She overheard and said, " No, we'll only bring one because one will live and one will die." This was a common belief.

We went to the hospital, and during the delivery, the twins were born in good condition. Dr. Ahmed Atta Hamouda supervised the delivery process. Afterward, the doctor asked my father to provide names for the babies so that birth certificates could be issued and they could be registered with the Ministry of Interior. My parents quickly consulted and agreed to name them Fadi and Moussa. However, Dr. Ahmed suggested naming them Fadi and Shadi. He explained that Fadi means the one who redeems and saves you with his soul or with any valuable thing he possesses, the rescuer from distress or hardship. Fadi, among Christians, is the Christ who redeemed humans with his precious blood. That's why people associate Fadi with redemption and saviorship. As for Shadi, it's a masculine Arabic name derived from Arabic roots. Shadi refers to the singer or the one who chants and sings, and it's also used for a student of knowledge and literature. In child-rearing, everyone used to help my mother because I was much calmer compared to my brother Fadi, and the proof of that is what my mother says, "My uncle Ziad used to refuse to carry Fadi because he was mischievous and said, 'I want to carry and play with Shadi.'"

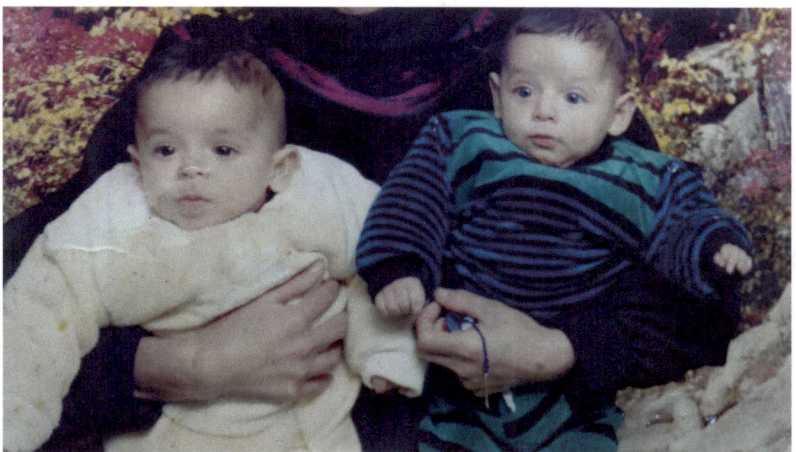

Fadi and Shadi in their mother's arms

Days passed quickly, and life took us through kindergarten and school together. The school system in Gaza involved registering and enrolling in school first. Then, at the beginning of the academic year, all students would gather in the courtyard, and the teacher would call out, for example, "First-grade Class 1," then call all the students who would join this class, and so on. Most of the time, my brother and I were in different classes, so we would go to the school principal and request to be in the same class. If she didn't agree, our father or mother would accompany us the next day to persuade the principal to agree. I don't remember much from this stage, but what I recall is that the classes were mixed between boys and girls but separated inside the classroom, which was unusual for us due to the traditions and culture of society. I remember we used to share the school expenses, and my brother would take them, and during break time, I would search for him among hundreds of students, and usually, we would agree on a meeting place, then I would go to the cafeteria to buy a sandwich and juice.

I don't remember much about what happened inside the classroom, but I was one of the best students, while my brother Fadi's performance was somewhat weak. When a teacher complained about my brother, it would come through me, and I felt sad because Fadi would be punished by our father for his shortcomings. My mother used to buy clothes for both of us, so we would wear the same clothes with only a slight difference in color. And all I remember is how beautiful it was, its beauty in every detail, innocence, playfulness, friendship, warmth, humility, honesty, sincerity, generosity, participation, and respect.

Fadi and Shadi, the twins who shared almost everything, were a vivid example of the close bond that signifies unity and integration in a world of differences. Although we spent many years together, the details of that time have become somewhat hazy, yet the memories of the conflicts between us remain vivid in my mind.

Harmony between us was not always easy. Despite sharing the same clothes, our desires and preferences often clashed. I remember how we would argue over color choices for different occasions, and those small disputes felt like storms in our little world. To everyone around us, we were a picture of brotherly harmony, but the reality was different, as each of us sought to distinguish ourselves amidst the sea of sameness.

As a child, I often felt that everything was divided into halves: school expenses, clothing, and sometimes even emotional attention. This sense of division was not easy, especially when I heard the women around us wishing for twins, which seemed like a blessing they desired while it felt like an additional burden for us.

Perhaps our family's financial situation deepened these feelings. My father worked under challenging conditions in the occupied territories, shifting between tough jobs like paving streets and picking fruits such as peaches, mangoes, and olives. These daily struggles became a part of our lives and taught us to share life in all its aspects, no matter how difficult or complex. In the end, those memories are an inseparable part of our family history, teaching us much about the balance between unity and difference.

I vividly remember those days when our streets were filled with sand, not yet paved, and cars were rare, while carts driven by donkeys filled the streets. As children, we spent most of our time playing and having fun, and sometimes we would sit and talk about our innocent dreams. Our school operated on a two-shift system: a morning shift that started at seven o'clock and ended at eleven-thirty, and an afternoon shift that began at twelve and finished at four. I vividly remember those days when we would go to school in our crisp uniforms, rushing back home to change into our play clothes.

The moments after school were the most eagerly awaited, as we gathered in the dusty courtyards to indulge in our favorite games. Football was one of those games, but it wasn't the only one. Amber was a special favorite. This game required forming two teams, each using simple protective gear like plastic or wooden boards. We would place a medium-sized bottle in the middle of the field and take turns throwing the ball to knock it down. If a team failed to knock it over, it would be the other team's turn. After the bottle was knocked down, a new round of excitement began as everyone ran around, passing the ball to try and hit members of the opposing team.

Another game we played with great enthusiasm was "Fishing". This game involved a ball, and the goal was to throw the ball with your hands at the others. Whoever got hit by the ball was out of the game, and the competition continued until only one player was left standing.

These games were more than just fun; they filled our lives with energy and taught us the values of teamwork and healthy competition. Our moments together were filled with laughter and excitement, and those memories remain etched in our minds as the most beautiful chapters of our childhood, telling a story of innocence and simplicity in a time that knew no boundaries or barriers.

I remember that we used to collect school expenses from friends to share in making breakfast or going on a trip. I remember the simplicity that surrounded us. One evening, I went to the mosque for the Maghrib prayer, and the atmosphere was filled with tranquility and spirituality. After the prayer, I met some friends who had a delightful idea. They suggested that we gather some simple food from our homes, such as olives, thyme, cheese, bread, and a teapot. We would then head to a nearby hilltop and have dinner together.

We set off towards the hilltop, where the surroundings were serene and the nature breathtaking. There, amidst the fresh air and under a starry sky, we spread our blankets and laid out the modest meal. The simple food, prepared with our own hands, brought us together in moments of joy and relaxation, away from the everyday worries of life. We sat together, sharing stories and laughter, savoring the flavors of our humble meal.

That evening, the hill became a witness to moments of warmth and friendship, as our voices mingled with the breeze and the city lights shimmered in the distance. It was a wonderful experience that filled our hearts with nostalgia for the simplicity of life and the beauty of human connections.

In high school, which is between the ages of 16, 17, 18, it was the first time my brother and I didn't meet in the same class. In this stage, I started to become myself and set a dream and goal to achieve. I aimed to rank second or third in this stage. I learned barbering because my father was a barber, and I hated this profession because I looked forward to progressing and joining university to dedicate my life to knowledge. I remember my father agreeing with a skilled and well-known barber for me to learn from him, but I only went once, and in other times, I spent time on the street to avoid learning barbering. I had many friends; we would sometimes gather to study and sometimes stay up late. I was loved among my peers, and everyone shared their secrets and aspirations with me. I remember once we were sitting at my house, and sometimes at another friend's house, and so on. And because the number of friends was many, some parents began to feel that we were wasting time, so our meetings together became undesirable by the parents. I remember my mother's friend came and said to me, "I asked Ahmed 'my friend' why he didn't accompany anyone except Shadi," I said to her, "I'm happy with that, but the other friends are good too." My friends' fathers felt that if their sons accompanied me, they wouldn't worry about his behavior or ethics because I was very well-mannered. There's an Arabic saying that goes, "Tell me who you accompany, and I'll tell you who you are." In this stage, the first battle with the occupation army occurred, which is the Battle of Furqan, which I will talk about in the fourth chapter.

The joyous atmosphere of a family celebrating success in high school

In 2010, we transitioned to the stage of secondary education, which precedes university education. I was enrolled in the scientific branch, the toughest among the branches, as it allows for studying human medicine and scientific specializations. However, my ambition was to study English language, so I decided to switch to the literary branch, which was relatively easier. This period was unstable and very tense because my father did not want me to switch to the literary branch. Unfortunately, my father was ignorant about university education because he had not attended it himself.

I remember the day of the results, a day when all students celebrate their success in this stage, and it's considered a festive day with the distribution of sweets, visits, and congratulations. The Ministry of Education announced that Monday would be the day of the result's announcement. I recall waking up shortly before the scheduled time, only to have a relative call out, "Congratulations, Shadi, on your success in secondary school." I asked about my GPA, and they said it was 87%. I graduated from this year with a GPA of 82%, which was very good and allowed me to study the English language.

I went on a visit to some universities with my uncle to familiarize myself with them and their other majors. I was happy that I had completed the school stage, with all its early waking up, school uniform, home-

My friends and me at the Islamic University of Gaza

18

work, and other school requirements. It was a beautiful stage with all its details, despite the hardships, effort, and exhaustion it entailed. I remember the professors, friends, library, buildings, classrooms, cafeteria, and gatherings. Despite my family's economic circumstances, my father left me money beside me while I slept. I used to spend a long time walking to save some money or to have enough for transportation to university.

The first year was challenging because it was the beginning and differed entirely from secondary school. What made it even more challenging was the increased number of courses per semester, and all the teaching was in English without translation. I felt exhausted during this period, but I did not give up until I graduated in 2014 with a very good GPA.

Dr. Kamelin Shatt, the President of the Islamic University, and me at the graduation ceremony

Life after graduation wasn't easy, especially with the prevalent belief that a degree holder was no different from someone who hadn't pursued education. There was a popular saying I often heard during that time: "تيتي تيتي زي ما رحتي زي ما جيتي" or "What goes around comes around." It's a whimsical and rhythmic phrase conveying the idea that someone's actions or behaviors can't be predicted or consistent. Despite this, I fought and struggled, starting to teach English in various educational centers. Opportunities were diverse, and I was diligent. I had a strong desire and passion to secure scholarships for further studies abroad, even making it twice to the shortlist for a Fulbright scholarship. In the end, I decided to stay and work in Gaza.

"Every hardworking person gets their share" summarizes this period, and I've said it repeatedly. You have to set goals for yourself and learn to rely on yourself while benefiting from others' experiences. In September 2016, I established the first English library, one of the proudest achievements. The idea arose from the scarcity of books, especially in English, in Gaza. So, a friend and I decided to work on this idea to serve all educated students, providing them a place to nurture their minds through reading and engaging in beneficial activities, enhancing the culture of libraries and reading within our Palestinian society, which lacks such initiatives.

Library activities

Initially, it wasn't easy due to the severe blockade on Gaza and the difficulty in obtaining books and donations from abroad. But with determination and hard work, dreams become reality. When I delivered the opening speech, I felt on top of the world because I created something that not only benefited me but also everyone living in Gaza. When I returned home after several days of preparation and exhaustion, I found a dedicated page for Beit Lahia city, everyone sharing the joy of this beautiful opening, expressing gratitude. In the end, they wrote, "We now have a library," and it became a trend in my city. I can't forget the friends, both from Gaza and abroad, who supported and encouraged us. Without their generous giving and encouragement, my dream wouldn't have come true. This project is still ongoing, serving many children and youth with diverse and beneficial activities.

In 2020, I got married, and my wife and I welcomed our first child, named Muhammad after my father. I'll delve further into this in the fourth chapter. Three years later, we were blessed with another child, Massa. Fadi got married a year after I did and had two children, Ibrahim and Sham.

Similarly, my sisters got married and also had two children. It says fate decreed that we would have the same thing.

Shadi with his children, Mohammad and Masa

3. Stories Behind the Wall

In 2006, legislative elections took place, the first and last time I witnessed such an event as I hadn't reached the legal age to participate. I remember it well, as I used to go to some schools where voters gathered and people would give them some guidance. All of this felt like I was brimming with vitality during my teenage years. Hamas won the elections, and after that, everything changed. The blockade was imposed on us, and everything felt constricted from all directions. I remember back then electricity only came for a few hours, and we relied on candles. We used to study under candlelight, surrounded by darkness from all sides.

One day, I heard the news of our neighbor's house burning down, not far from us. It burned down with everyone inside. I went to see the burnt house that day, and the father was talking about what happened. He said the children were playing together, and his younger son went to buy some sweets. They lit a candle and fell asleep, and then the fire started, consuming them all. No one survived.

Graduates walked the streets, unsure of their destination due to the high unemployment rate, the abundance of graduates, and the intense competition for jobs. I always wondered what the future held for us. Would my fate be like those graduates after all these hardships? Eventually, we found ourselves hanging our certificates and looking at them with a burning heart, wondering whether to pursue demanding jobs that barely cover personal expenses.

We spent most of our nights by candlelight. If you wanted to go out and walk in the streets at night, you wouldn't see anyone except for the light of cars or mobile phones.

Traveling was not in our vocabulary during this time because the Rafah crossing, the only gateway through which we could see the outside world, was closed and rarely opened throughout the year.

The Persistence of Dream

The atmosphere was tense in Gaza, the territory living under continuous siege for years. Amidst this complex situation, Mohammed was born, an ambitious young man in his early twenties, who dreamed of becoming a doctor since his childhood. His dark eyes spoke of a sincere desire to serve his community and to help those who suffer under the siege.

However, the blockade was not just a physical barrier, but also a psychological obstacle. Mohammed couldn't travel outside the territory to pursue his university studies due to strict restrictions on the movement of people and goods. Nevertheless, his determination remained unshaken, and he continued to search for ways to achieve his dream.

The Power of Hope

Lina, a young Palestinian mother, was one of the strong women living in Gaza under the siege. After losing her husband to airstrikes, she found herself responsible for caring for her four children and facing life's challenges alone. Despite the difficult financial circumstances and limited resources, her heart was full of love and strength, and her determination to provide a decent life for her children was unparalleled.

In the face of adversity, Lina drew strength from her love for her children and worked hard to provide them with food, shelter, and healthcare. She sacrificed everything for them, bearing the heavy burden of responsibility on her shoulders. With each passing day, her strength and determination grew, turning sorrow and pain into a driving force for success and optimism. In tough times, Lina always remembered her late husband's words: "Be strong, my dear, you will overcome everything." These words represented a beacon of hope for her in the darkness surrounding her.

The Will of Youth

Mahmoud, a determined Palestinian youth in his twenties, carried a big dream in his heart. He wanted to build a bright future for himself and his family in Gaza, despite the many challenges he faced. After completing high school, Mahmoud struggled to find employment due to the blockade, which significantly affected the local economy and increased unemployment rates.

Nevertheless, Mahmoud refused to surrender to the harsh conditions and decided to be an inspiration to other youth. He started looking for small job opportunities and small business projects he could start, and his strong willpower helped him overcome all obstacles. Mahmoud continued to develop his skills and gain new knowledge through training courses and workshops, and he worked hard to build a network of professional and social relationships to support him on his journey. Thanks to his patience and determination, Mahmoud succeeded in achieving some small victories, which gave him the confidence in his ability to achieve his dreams despite all the difficulties.

And so, Mahmoud continued on his journey towards achieving his goals, believing that hope still exists even in the toughest of circumstances. Despite all the challenges and hardships, he trusted that one day his dream would come true and he would make a better future for himself and his community.

"Nora" and her Battle with Cancer

In a small village in Gaza, lived Nora, a young woman in her early thirties, with her husband and three children. Nora lived a quiet and happy life, caring for her family and working hard to provide the best possible life for them. But everything changed in a moment, when she received a shocking diagnosis from the doctor.

Nora's ordeal began when she felt severe pain in her body, and as the pain intensified, she decided to visit the doctor. After a series of tests, the result was shocking: she was diagnosed with advanced breast cancer. This news was a great shock to Nora and her family, as they did not expect to face such a big challenge.

Nora was directed to the only cancer treatment center in the area, and the difficult battle with the disease began. Chemotherapy sessions and surgeries started, and Nora tried with all her might to withstand

and overcome the disease, for the sake of her children and for the sake of life.

However, the blockade imposed on Gaza made it difficult to obtain the necessary treatment and medications. Pharmacies suffered from supply shortages, and medical services were limited due to strict restrictions on the movement of individuals and goods. Despite all the difficulties, Nora continued her battle, trying with all her might to stay strong for her family and for herself. But despite all her efforts, her health deteriorated rapidly, and her hopes for recovery faded.

In the end, Nora passed away carrying an unfulfilled dream in her heart, leaving behind a grieving family and broken hearts. Her battle with cancer was a story of resilience and courage, of sacrifice and love that knows no bounds, and it was a lesson about the power of the human spirit in facing life's toughest challenges.

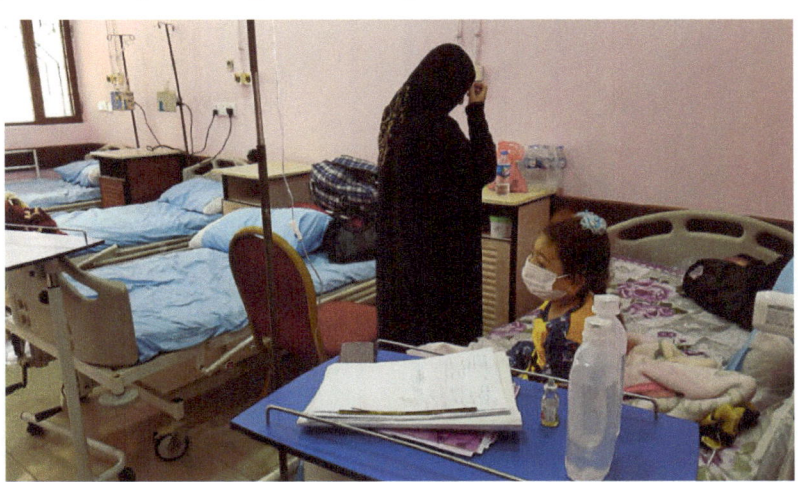

4. Loving Gaza

The Wedding

Palestinians have rituals and customs surrounding marriage that families strive to uphold and preserve despite occupation, displacement, exile, and pain, aiming to maintain the spirit and memory of a people aspiring for life.

While there may be slight differences in the appearance of marriage rituals and customs among Palestinians in Gaza, the West Bank, Palestinian citizens of Israel, and Palestinian refugees in Arab and Western countries, the origin of these customs is the same, and most Palestinians endeavor to maintain them as much as possible.

The first step is the selection of the bride: Typically, the task of choosing the bride is entrusted to the groom's mother. In Palestine, there is no formal system of engagement. If the young man does not have a close female relative like a cousin, aunt, or niece whom he wishes to marry, his mother, along with her friends and relatives, compile a list of girls interested in marrying him, based on his criteria and the specifications he sets for his life partner. When the young man chooses a girl, his mother visits the girl's house and asks for her hand on behalf of her son.

It is customary for Palestinian families to give the bride's family a grace period to inquire about the groom and his family, his morals, religion, and integrity. After the grace period elapses, the groom's mother returns to the girl's house to hear the response. If the response is positive, a day is set for the groom to see his bride, and for the bride to see her groom.

On the appointed day, the groom and his parents visit the bride's house, where they are welcomed by the bride's family in the presence of her uncles and brothers. The bride enters, carrying coffee, greets the guests, and sits for a while to see the groom and for him to see her, often in a separate room with one of the bride's brothers present. During this meeting, the dowry may be discussed, or the matter may be left for a few days.

Then, a group of family elders and influential figures return to the bride's house, formally requesting her hand in marriage. Discussions begin about the dowry, deferred payment, and household furnishings, among other matters. Dowries vary between families, whether immediate or deferred. The agreed-upon currency for the dowry is the Jordanian Dinar, ranging from 2000 to 5000 dinars, to allow the bride to buy gold, clothes, or other necessities.

After reaching an agreement between the groom's representatives and the bride's family, a day is set for what is called in our tradition "the day of engagement," during which the immediate dowry is paid to the bride. Friends, relatives, and neighbors are invited to the bride's house, where sweets, typically baklava or knafeh, along with soft drinks and plain coffee, are served. This marks the first formal and public step of the wedding process.

Later, the marriage contract is signed, either at the bride's house with the presence of a marriage official, or the couple may go to the Sharia court, where the marriage contract is signed before a legal judge, ensuring the bride's consent to the marriage. This step is the most legitimate and binding between the spouses. After the marriage contract, there is a stage called "al-Samda," which is an engagement ceremony attended by the closest relatives of the bride and groom. It involves announcing the engagement and presenting gifts and sweets.

In Palestinian culture, even after the marriage contract, it is usually not allowed for the bride and groom to be alone together in private or public places without the company of a relative, as Palestinian society is conservative. However, this varies from one family to another.

The engagement period can last from 3 to 6 months, typically. After several months, the wedding date is agreed upon by both parties. The groom prepares himself, arranges the marital home, reserves the wedding hall, and prints the invitations, distributing them to guests.

The wedding night is called "the night of henna," whether for the groom or the bride. Before the wedding night, the groom invites friends to a bachelor party, while the bride invites her friends and relatives to bid her farewell and hold a small party for her.

The following day, another celebration takes place, known as "Zaffa Day." In the morning, a meal of rice and meat or chicken is prepared for the guests, including relatives and neighbors. Two hours later, the Zaffa procession begins, with all the groom's friends and relatives participating. They decorate their cars, especially the bride and groom's car, with flowers and garlands, and traditional music is played as they head to the bride's house to take her and her family. Then, they all proceed in a grand procession, honking their horns, parading through the streets, taking a tour of beautiful spots while inside their cars. They eventually return to the wedding hall, where festivities typically begin at p.m. and end around 10 p.m. Afterward, the bride and groom move to their new home to start a beautiful life together and form a family.

Naming Children

Palestinians have traditionally adhered to certain rituals and customs when naming their firstborn child, often naming them after the paternal grandfather. If the grandfather is deceased, it was common in the past to avoid naming the child after a living grandfather, as it was considered a bad omen foretelling the grandfather's death. However, in the last three decades, it has become customary for a man to name his son after himself, following a prevalent tradition. A son is usually named after his father only if the father passed away shortly before or after the son's birth, symbolizing the replacement of one man with another. Sometimes, a man may choose to name his children after beloved family members, prominent figures in the community, or political leaders.

Many Palestinian families prefer to name their children after prophets, righteous saints, companions of the Prophet Muhammad, or with names starting with "Abd" followed by one of the beautiful names of Allah. For girls, there is a preference for names similar to those of righteous women such as the Prophet's wives and companions. Christian Palestinian communities may also name boys after prophets like Elias, Jesus,

George, and John, while girls might be named Hannah and Mary. Other non-religious names given to children often reflect characteristics such as strength and courage, like Tiger, Wolf, and Lion for boys, or Joy and Smiles to signify happiness and joy.

Traditionally, the seventh day following a child's birth marks the day of naming. On this day, the child's hair is typically cut for the first time. A sacrifice known as "Aqiqah" is offered, with one sheep slaughtered for a girl and two for a boy. This celebration can take place on the seventh, fourteenth, twenty-first, twenty-eighth, or thirty-fifth day after the child's birth. Additionally, the weight of the child's hair is measured, and an equivalent amount of silver is distributed as charity. Nowadays, children are often named on the day of their birth.

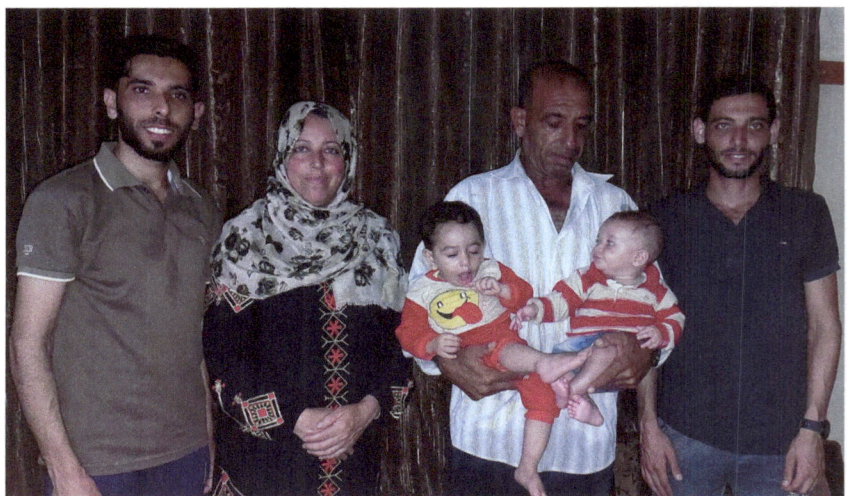

Death

When a member of the Palestinian community passes away, the family of the deceased announces the news, and many people participate in the funeral procession. Relatives, neighbors, and friends then visit the family's home or the mourning tent to offer condolences. During the mourning period, relatives, neighbors, and friends provide food for the family of the deceased. During the condolences, special phrases are said, such as "May God increase your reward," "May God accept your efforts," and "May you find patience." In rural areas of Palestine, neighboring villages are informed of the death, and their participation in mourning may vary slightly from city to city, with some cities having a three-day mourning period for men and one day for women.

As for my hometown Beit Lahia, which was formerly known as the city of generosity and leisure, it was renowned for its vast agricultural lands cultivated with delicious citrus fruits, and vegetables, in addition to its geographical fame. However, it was also known for its noble qualities associated with its inhabitants who have lived there for decades.

The Palestinian city of Beit Lahia, often described as the "Garden of Gaza," is located in the northern part of the Gaza Strip, approximately seven kilometers north of Gaza City. It is bordered by the occupied village of Hirbiya to the north, the Mediterranean Sea to the west, Jabalia to the south, and Beit Hanoun to the east. The city covers an area of approximately 24,500 dunums, of which about 14,374 dunums fall under municipal jurisdiction.

Before the Nakba of 1948, Beit Lahia was among the largest Palestinian villages in the Gaza District in terms of land area and property owner-ship. Its lands once extended across neighboring areas and villages such as Beit Hanoun, Deir Sunayd, Damra, Najd, and Simsim, reaching the outskirts of the town of Bureir to the east, while the village of Hirbiya marked its northern boundary. Today, the population of Beit Lahia is estimated at around 75,000 people. The city is surrounded by sand dunes, some of which rise up to approximately 55 meters above sea level, and it has long been known for its agricultural character, green belts, and large trees that form an integral part of its landscape and collective memory.

Although Beit Lahia now contains numerous public facilities and govern-ment institutions alongside what remains of its green lands, it has retained social and cultural characteristics that distinguish its people from those of other cities—traits that emerge clearly in times of both joy and sorrow.

.One beautiful custom preserved by its people is the tradition of solidarity and compassion. As soon as they hear of someone's death in the city, they rush to leave whatever they have in their hands to be with the deceased's family. This support doesn't stop there. Once the deceased is buried, they rush back to their homes to take food prepared by their wives to offer condolences. They carry it on their heads and go to the mourning house. Their actions speak to their belief that the mourners cannot afford to feed themselves during this time of grief, so they take it upon themselves to provide them with food, as a gesture of assistance and comfort. This food isn't sourced from fancy restaurants or large stores but rather from the humble fridge of a poor household or a simple home in desperate need of this meal. Yet, it's the tradition inherited from Prophet Muhammad that makes people prioritize others even if they themselves are in dire need. They gather thyme, oil, olives, cheese, and some eggs from their modest homes to adorn a single plate, denying themselves in favor of their grieving neighbor.

In some cities like Nablus, on the third day of mourning, there is a custom called "Dalail" that is practiced, which is not present in other cities today. After the afternoon prayer, on the third day of mourning for the deceased, the family and relatives gather at the deceased's house or at the family's meeting place, if any, or at the mourning house. They read a portion of the Quran, one or two chapters depending on the number of attendees, then distribute sweets to the mourners, usually knafeh.

Another tradition related to death is the forty-day memorial, where the same rituals of Dalail are performed. The forty-day memorial is prevalent in most areas, but recently, it has become common to donate money to a mosque or to the poor instead of distributing food. There is also the "First Eid" where families gather again on the first holiday after the death of the deceased. During the mid-morning period before the noon prayer, condolences are offered only to the family of the deceased. Alternatively, the relatives of the deceased stay up at the deceased's house on the night before the holiday. In some areas, on the third day of mourning, sacrifices are made, and dinner is provided for the attendees, known as "Al-Khatma."

Each tradition has a set of customs that must be followed by both young and old in the community to maintain the social order, any deviation from which could lead to its collapse. For example, some of the customs and traditions regarding mourning were considered essential, and violating them was seen as a disrespect to the deceased and their family. For instance, suspending expressions of joy in the village for a period of forty days, especially if the deceased was young, refraining from wearing new clothes, women not adorning themselves, and men not grooming themselves. Nowadays, this tradition has narrowed to be limited to the family of the deceased, their friends, and neighbors. If a family member has an upcoming joyous event, it may be postponed for a long period, sometimes up to a year. Sweets are not made by the family of the deceased on holidays, and congratulatory visits are not accepted.

In the past, clothes were not washed for forty days, and important dishes were not cooked. But recently, this custom has disappeared.

Dialectal Diversity

Despite the small size of the Gaza Strip, you'll find a variety of dialects, reflecting the cultural, social, and historical diversity of its inhabitants. The region is characterized by several local dialects that differ in pronunciation, vocabulary, and grammatical rules, stemming from various factors that have influenced the evolution of language in the area. While Gaza's dialects share many common features, each has its own unique characteristics that distinguish it from the others. For example, the urban dialect in Gaza may differ from the dialect in rural areas or refugee camps. These different dialects in Gaza reflect the social diversity of the region, with residents coming from different backgrounds such as farmers, Bedouins, and refugees, each carrying their own linguistic and cultural heritage.

Allow me to mention the dialect of my hometown Beit Lahia, where we use the "kasra" (i.e., the short vowel "i") at the beginning of a word, for example, "jameela" with a "kasra" whereas in other dialects, it might be pronounced with a "fatha" (i.e., the short vowel "a"). Additionally, there may be differences in some phrases, such as "ma shufet hash" meaning "I haven't seen it" in our dialect, whereas in other dialects, they might use "ma shufet huwsh."

What distinguishes the dialect of Beit Lahia from others is the elongation of the vowel in the word. This is because most of its residents are citizens rather than refugees, as they are the original inhabitants of the city. And if you hear someone you know is from Beit Lahia say "ya ghurab," it's a sign that something unpleasant or undesirable has happened. This indicates that the crow is a symbol of pessimism. One day I asked my grandmother about this, and she said, "The crow was a symbol of pessimism for the Ottomans." They lived with us for a period of time, and this is what was borrowed from them.

The beauty of dialectal diversity lies in its ability to add depth and richness to language, providing unique interpretations and expressions. Moreover, it reflects the integration and peaceful coexistence among different cultures and groups within society. For example, dialects can be a source of pride and belonging for individuals and groups, representing their personal and collective identity and history.

Furthermore, interaction between dialects enhances communication and understanding among members of society, even in times of disagreement and diversity. It contributes to building bridges of respect and tolerance among people, fostering a sense of cooperation and solidarity.

5. My Journey During the Wars

Under the sky of Gaza, amidst the rubble of homes and the sound of exploding shells, life found itself defying harsh conditions, with hope sprouting amidst the walls of destruction. Those were the days where screams mingled with the call to prayer, where the sound of waves merged with the sound of weeping. It was there that my journey through wars began. In this chapter of my memoirs, I will narrate a personal story, one not written in numbers and statistics, but in the language of the soul and experiences. These are the days that won't easily fade from my memory.

It's a story about learning to survive and endure under difficult circumstances, and how hope can flourish in barren land. All this and more I found in my journey through the wars in Gaza. My journey will be filled with painful scenes and tough moments, but it will also be rich with sacrifice, courage, and the struggles of many who lived under the skies of Gaza during difficult times. I will tell you stories brimming with life and lessons, and I will try with every word to convey my feelings, experiences, and the experiences of others, so that you understand the meaning of resilience and hope in the face of adversity. About the hope born amidst the rubble of destruction, and about the great sacrifices made by people to protect their families and loved ones.

It's a personal journey, but it's also the story of all the people who lived under the shadows of wars, in Gaza and in other places in the world. Let's embark on this journey filled with honest details and genuine emotions, to take a deep look at what it means to live under the skies of Gaza during wars.

2008-2009 Battle of Al-Furqan / Operation Cast Lead

At the end of the eleventh-grade chapter in high school, specifically after finishing the English language exam and on my way home, I heard intense shelling near our area, which was the first time we witnessed such a thing. The Battle of Al-Furqan, also known as Operation Cast Lead by the Israelis, which took place in Gaza in 2008-2009, was one of the most significant horrors in the history of the Palestinian-Israeli conflict. The confrontations began on December 27, 2008. During the battle, Israel launched intense air and ground attacks, using internationally banned weapons such as white phosphorus and depleted uranium, and detonated over a thousand tons of explosives causing massive destruction to infrastructure and properties in the Gaza Strip, in addition to devastating losses of civilian lives. The death toll and casualties among Palestinians were significant, with estimates indicating that over 1,400 Palestinians were killed, including many women and children, and over 5,000 wounded.

Children were among the most affected victims of the conflict. Many families witnessed the loss of their children due to Israeli airstrikes, and many other children suffered severe injuries or the loss of their family members. These stories highlight the innocence sacrificed by children in the midst of the conflict. Among these children were my neighbors Jihad and Shadi Ghubn, who were playing in our neighborhood when a rocket fell on them, shattering everything around them. I rushed out of the house to help and found my friend carrying Shadi whose body was torn in half, and Jihad was injured. Shadi, the gentle soul loved by everyone who knew him, was gone forever.

In the heart of the chaos and destruction caused by the fierce and barbaric war, there was an unforgettable day, a day when I asked my mother to stay one night at my uncle's house. When I arrived at my uncle's house, the atmosphere was tense with anxiety and worries. The shelling was intensifying from all sides, and the terrifying sound of shells was shaking the ground and echoing in the horizon. At this difficult time, internationally banned white phosphorus began to rain from the sky like fiery rain, and fires were consuming everything in their path. As we tried to stay alive, we witnessed moments of extreme terror, where the fires almost engulfed us entirely. We saw death more than once on that hot and terrifying night, but by the grace of God, we miraculously survived that potential calamity.

Many civilian families fled their destroyed homes in search of safe shelter to protect them from the dangers of killing and destruction. The streets were crowded with fleeing people, carrying whatever little belongings they could and their young children, while searching for temporary shelter that would provide them with protection.

In every direction, there were cries of frightened children and women, and the faces of men bearing the burden of protecting their families amidst this chaos and terror. Those moments were filled with panic and anxiety, as everyone knew that danger lurked around every corner.

Gaza witnessed massive destruction of infrastructure, including homes, schools, hospitals, government facilities, and economic establishments. This destruction greatly impacted people's lives and their economy, increasing their suffering and the difficulty of rebuilding their lives after the end of the battle.

The aggression lasted for 23 days, and the battle ended with a cease-fire on January 18, 2009, after intense international pressure to halt the escalation. Although the declared goal of the Israeli operation was to stop rocket fire from Gaza, the massive destruction caused by that operation raised widespread international criticism and raised questions about the human and material cost of the war on Palestinians in Gaza.

2012: Pillar of Cloud / Operation Pillar of Defense

On November 14, 2012, the Battle of Pillar of Cloud ignited in the Gaza Strip, leading to escalating clashes between Palestinians and Israelis, resulting in massive human and material losses. Those days were filled with tension and fear, as the humanitarian crisis worsened amidst intense shelling and ground attacks by the Israeli army on the Gaza Strip. The battle began with escalating tensions between the parties after the assassination of Hamas' military wing leader, Ahmed al-Jabari, by Israel, which sparked this battle. Clashes erupted throughout the Strip, with border areas, cities, and villages witnessing mutual attacks with rockets and missiles.

Civilian facilities and infrastructure in Gaza suffered severe damage from continuous shelling, leading to the displacement of thousands of families and the destruction of many homes, schools, and hospitals. The streets were filled with debris and rubble, and people lived in a state of terror and despair, with water and electricity cuts and a shortage of medical supplies.

After 8 days of bloody confrontations and intense shelling, a temporary ceasefire agreement was reached through Egyptian mediation. Thus, the Battle of Pillar of Cloud in Gaza ended, leaving behind unforgettable traces and losses, and destruction that would take years to rebuild and repair.

2014: Battle of the Withered Grain / Operation Protective Edge

The Battle of the Withered Grain is considered one of the most tragic battles in the history of the Palestinian-Israeli conflict. This battle represented the peak of the long-awaited tension and violence, as Israeli occupation forces amassed in massive numbers on the borders of the Gaza Strip, ready to launch a wide-scale attack on Palestinian areas.

The sky was filled with gray clouds, with the sound of warplanes echoing in the horizon, announcing the coming storm. Mortar shells and rockets scattered on Palestinian land like rain, sometimes exploding in the air and causing violent explosions, and sometimes crashing into the ground, leaving traces of destruction and devastation.

On July 8, Israel decided to launch a comprehensive attack, naming it Operation Protective Edge, and referred to by Hamas as "The Eaten Storm." The declared Israeli objective was to stop Palestinian rocket fire towards Israel and deter further attacks. The war evolved in three stages.

2023-2024: Operation Al-Aqsa Flood

When I left Gaza and headed to Malaysia to attend a training course, I didn't expect to experience such a level of difficulty and hardship. Throughout that period was far from my family and loved ones, and war was raging in my country, leaving my loved ones facing difficulties and suffering.

Days and weeks passed, and I was still there, away from the bombardment and the cries of children and the sighs of women. The news reaching me from home carried the cruelty of reality and the bitterness of events. The people of northern Gaza were suffering from blockade and food shortages, forced to resort to eating animals such as fodder and grass to survive.

At the same time, events on the ground were escalating, with cities and villages subjected to continuous shelling by soldiers and tanks. Families found themselves trapped in their homes, with fear and anxiety gripping their hearts, and with no safe haven to turn to.

During those moments, longing and anxiety gnawed at my heart, wondering about the fate of my loved ones and how they were coping with these difficult circumstances. Hopes weighed heavily on my heart, and prayer was the only weapon I held to cast into the sky, hoping it would find its way to my loved ones and protect them from harm.

At that time, amid all these challenges and suffering, I learned patience and endurance, and realized the value of hope and faith. That experience was truly impactful, as war taught me that strength lies not only in fighting, but in the ability to persevere and remain optimistic in the face of adversity.

My Little Home

After graduating from university with a degree in English language teaching, I began to explore new horizons of matters I hadn't thought about before, such as building an apartment, finding a job, and getting married. The beginning of my new journey was work, where I started teaching the English language in several educational centers, and I had the ability to present information in a new way, attracting many students to enroll in the courses I offered.

I enjoyed teaching advanced levels like high school and university. I can't say I enjoyed direct praise from students, but I felt their appreciation through their presentation of their views and their interest in the lessons.

Among the beautiful stories I want to share is the story of a student by the name Nasiba Ghanem. Nasiba enrolled in some of the courses as I offered to teach various levels of the English language, and she was in high school. Although she was one of the weak students academically, she was diligent and wanted to improve her level in English. She always attended classes and asked probing questions.

One day, my aunt Jameela, who had studied Islamic law at the university for a while, got married and had five children, decided to join us at the university to study the English language. She wanted to improve her language skills to be able to teach her children and increase her chances for job opportunities. And English was very important in Gaza, where parents cared about teaching it to their children from elementary stages.

In the first semester, my aunt Jameela faced many difficulties in studying English and excelling over her classmates. She started asking questions to the successful students about how to improve their language skills, and she tried to benefit from their experiences. And once, when my aunt asked one of the successful students about how to learn English, Nasiba answered her saying: "You are from the Salem family, aren't you?" My aunt replied: "Yes," so Nasiba answered: "Ask Shadi," My aunt asked with surprise: "What do you mean?" So Nasiba answered: "I used to hate English, but when I studied with Shadi, I loved the language and I did not expect to study this specialization before, but here I am and I am the first in the batch in this specialization."

When my aunt shared this story with me, I felt joy and pride because I felt that I made a difference in someone's life, and her life changed thanks to learning the English language.

After 5 years of tiredness, exhaustion, and a limited salary, I started building a small apartment. The apartment was like a little paradise in a world full of chaos and noise. In the corners of the narrow apartment,

memories came to life, filling the air with the scent of joy and hope. Every wall hid behind it a different story, and every corner held a beautiful memory dancing to the rhythm of time.

There were unforgettable moments, like those quiet nights my wife and I spent in the candlelight, where conversation flowed between us like an endless river, exchanging laughter and dreams like flowers exchange breezes.

Every morning, the windows of the apartment shone with the bright rays of the sun, refreshing the rooms with its warmth and radiating hope and life in every corner. Those bright days carried promises of a bright future, where we dreamed of building a family and achieving our dreams together.

And when the moment of marriage came, the apartment turned into a magical place, adorned with the colors of joy and celebration. Those moments resembled a beautiful artistic painting, where the voices of the guests mingled with the innocent voices of the children, and the lights and colors danced together in an unforgettable wedding party.

And with the arrival of the children, the apartment became warmer and more loving, as the rooms filled with the sounds of laughter, crying, and the first steps of the first child. Those precious moments reflected the greatest hopes and aspirations, as we wished for our children success and happiness in a life filled with love and prosperity.

But, with the arrival of the war and the shells of the battle, everything changed. Our beautiful dream turned into a nightmare, and the small apartment that was a safe haven for us turned into a devastated square. Nevertheless, those beautiful memories will remain alive in our hearts, to remind us of the happy times and to strengthen our determination to build a better future despite all the difficulties.

Echoes of Innocence: The Story of Hamoud in the Shadow of War

After just three months of building the bonds of marriage, the news of my wife's pregnancy came like a delicate flower in the field of life. However, it was her first experience, a difficult pregnancy and a challenging ordeal she endured greatly in the early months.

Nights of pain disrupted the peace of sleep, as I watched over her with renewed concern, bearing the weight of her worries and pains on my shoulders as I wandered through the whirlwind of fatigue to my workplace.

At the beginning of the ninth month, an invitation came from her family for an outdoor excursion, a beautiful day filled with joy and happiness. But at its end, fate intervened, and I suffered a painful foot fracture. I went to the hospital, where the fracture was diagnosed without the need for a cast, but I learned that I couldn't walk on my feet.

The next morning, my wife's pains returned, and she was in the expected period of delivery. I hurried to my mother downstairs and told her, "It seems Nora is going to give birth today." I requested a car to transport her to the hospital, and despite the pain in my foot that had not yet subsided, I was by her side every step of the way.

I entered the dark delivery room and remained in the waiting room, my heart tense and anxious for the awaited moment of birth. And when the blessed cries shook me, my mother-in-law informed me with immense joy that our son, Mohammed, (affectionately known as Hamoud') was born, and he was well.

Those fleeting beautiful moments embodied the wonder of fatherhood as I held my son in my hands for the first time. I felt an indescribable joy fill my heart as I realized in that beautiful moment that I was a father for the first time, ready to face all the challenges of life for him.

When a person becomes a parent for the first time, their heart embraces feelings they've never felt before, and everything in their life changes dramatically. The feeling of fatherhood for the first time is mixed with joy, worry, and tension, as it is an exciting experience full of new responsibilities. My responsibility towards this little being who relies entirely on me for care and protection increased. There was a sense of pride in being present for the first time as a father, but at the same time, there was a constant sense of worry. Will I be able to meet his needs? Will I be a good father? Will I be able to provide everything he needs to grow and thrive?

Despite the mix of worry with joy, the moment of seeing my son for the first time was an unforgettable and enchanting moment. Feelings of tenderness and love engulfed me, and I felt my heart beating stronger than ever before. Since then, my journey as a father began with learning a lot, developing myself, forming a strong bond with my son, and providing the support and love he needed at every stage of his growth and development.

On a beautiful spring day, we gathered to celebrate his seventh-day celebration. The atmosphere was filled with joy and happiness, as the scent of incense mingled with the fragrance of roses, and the laughter of children and the sounds of congratulations filled every corner of the house.

It was an unforgettable day, a day where my heart surpassed the limits of joy, when Hamoud uttered his first sweet words, "Baba" and "Mama." That moment was a special time for the soul and mind, as dawn broke and joy filled our hearts, and laughter and happiness echoed in every corner of our home. The words "Baba" and "Mama" were the most precious gift Hamoud could give us that day, as if they were a love poem etched in the sky witnessing the beginning of a journey of giving and affection.

Days passed swiftly, and the day came when I had to leave Gaza, filled with longing and sorrow for the sake of building a brighter future for him and my family. I remember this day well, when Hamoud said to me with a voice full of longing, "Baba, I want to go with you," which added to my pain because he was very attached to me. Traveling from Gaza to the outside world is not easy under the suffocating blockade and long waiting periods. We travel from Gaza to Egypt on foot due to the fatigue and exhaustion we face at every checkpoint. The journey from Gaza to the Egyptian hall on the Egyptian side alone takes hours despite the short distance, which does not exceed ten minutes by car. And in the Egyptian hall, we wait for hours until our passports are stamped and we are allowed to enter.

Amid the genocide, my family moved after being demanded to evacuate by the Israeli army to shelter places, and when we say shelter places, they are not hotels or suitable places for people, but schools that have been bombed and destroyed. My family spent a school semester in an UNRWA school with three families in a space of no more than thirty-five meters. As you know, children love movement and it is difficult to stop them. There was a young man convulsing on the ground in the schoolyard, so Hamoud, my 3-year-old son, hurried to see what was happening. His grandmother saw him and asked him, "Why did you come?" Mohammed replied: "To see the dead person."

I asked myself, why do Palestinian children live like this? Shouldn't the last thing they learn be death? And why, why, why... I hope to find an answer.

Hamoud is at school. However, his school life did not begin there. Rather, he was displaced due to the brutal bombing and destruction that ruined everything. In November 2023, the second month of the war, Hamoud was looking forward to his birthday, so he said to his mother, "Mama, tomorrow is my birthday. Will we celebrate it by buying me a cake and candy? There are many children in this room who can celebrate with us." Despite the limited resources, his mother insisted on fulfilling his request and celebrating it. Hamoud celebrated his third birthday under bombardment, destruction, and killing, not knowing the meanings behind these words.

On one of the nights filled with bombardment, Hamoud woke up startled, crying and saying, "I want Baba, I want Baba, I want to go back home to play with my toys with Baba." Everyone was moved by Hamoud's crying, as those innocent words carried a deep pain, reopening wounds in the hearts and causing tears of longing and yearning. Children and adults alike cried amidst a silence pierced by broken dreams and grieving mothers' screams. Mothers wept for their innocent children, and fathers cried for the dream that vanished in the bleak fog of war.

In our small, beautiful city, the atmosphere was filled with joy and happiness during the holiday. The streets were adorned with lights and decorations, and every house emitted the scent of pastries and delicious sweets. Families gathered around lavish breakfast tables, exchanging congratulations and genuine laughter.

In this atmosphere of love and hope, children eagerly awaited the Eid-al-fitr. They woke up early in the morning, responding to the call of joy after a month of fasting and supplication. Children wore their finest clothes and decorated their hands with henna, ready to welcome the holiday with joy and splendor.

With the ringing of bells and the Eid prayer, everyone headed to mosques and public squares, responding to the call of prayer and glorification. After the prayer, celebrations and activities began, with children exchanging gifts and sweets, and smiles and laughter continuing abundantly.

But this year was different, as Hamoud and his family found themselves in shelters, under a roof of darkness and fear, amid the sounds of bombardment and destruction shaking the ground and rising into the sky. The usual joy of the holiday died in their hearts, killed by the missiles fired from all sides, and among the children who lost their toys destroyed by tank shells.

Little Hamoud continues to live the war within him, trapped between walls of darkness and screams of pain, in shelters and displacement sites where the suffering of the innocent is embodied. Hamoud and his family were forced to leave their home and belongings behind, seeking refuge under a roof of despair and growing hope.

The story of Hamoud and the suffering of children in the shadow of war may be saddening, but it also reflects the strength of will and resilience in the face of harsh conditions. Despite all the hardships, hope still resides in their hearts, and life retains the taste of hope and optimism, even in the toughest circumstances.

Let us all pray to create a better future for these children. Let the story of Hamoud and his suffering be a witness to injustice and oppression, and a catalyst for all of us to work towards ending wars and building a world of peace, justice, and equality for all children everywhere

Massa's First Year

The beloved beauty of my heart and the darling of everyone around her, Massa, with her beautiful face and wide green eyes. In the beginning of her arrival, I remember she used to love sleeping a lot, and without any movement, I would go and wake her up just to make sure she was alive. When I left for Malaysia, she was only 7 months old, and after a month, the war came. I couldn't imagine how it would be with my wife and the two children in these difficult times. I couldn't imagine her trying in every bombardment to hold them and comfort them so they would feel safe and their father away from them. At the beginning of the war, Massa was breastfeeding from her mother, and due to fear and destruction, her mother couldn't breastfeed her because of the dryness of milk in her mother's breast. Massa started crawling and her teeth came out, and her father was away from her in these beautiful moments. Massa says "Daddy" through hearing other children, and she also says "Daddy," but she doesn't see or know her father.

On 16 of Feb. 2024, my daughter, Massa, turned one year old. On a day like this, Massa came into the world. Imagine how joyful that day was and how sad this day is, given the indescribable circumstances we are in, which no human mind can fathom. What will I tell Massa when she grows up and asks me about her childhood and her first year on this earth? I won't lie, and I will tell her the truth, that she spent most of this year displaced, moving from one shelter to another just to survive. I will tell her about the nearly 100,000 casualties between martyrs and wounded, about our home that was completely bombed, where her bed and clothes were. I will tell her how we struggled to find food and milk just to feed her, and how her mother insisted on celebrating her birthday with the simplest things to make her happy and to bring joy to the children around her.

From Dreams to Tragedy: The Life and Loss of Mosab Al-Masri

When Mosab Al-Masri looked at his high school diploma, feeling pride and accomplishment, he didn't know that this small piece of paper would be the beginning of his simultaneously challenging and thrilling life story.

Mosab was born into a middle-class family, where his father worked diligently every day to provide enough money to keep the family stable. However, Mosab's love for knowledge and his great ambition drove him to pursue his education despite the significant financial challenges he faced.

After graduating from high school with distinction, Mosab joined university to study computer science, and here his real battle began. He dreamed of becoming an engineer and continuing his studies abroad to achieve this dream, but the harsh economic reality for his family was a major obstacle in his path.

Nevertheless, Mosab did not succumb to despair; instead, he continued to pursue his dreams with determination and perseverance. He worked hard alongside his studies, exerting his utmost effort to achieve the highest grades in university. Whenever he faced difficulty, he remembered his father's story, who borrowed money to provide him with the necessary expenses for his education. This memory was the motivation that kept him going.

The cursed war came, and Mosab and his family sought refuge at the UNRWA school, where my family is located, as a "safe place." He was injured yesterday morning and continued bleeding until he was martyred in the evening due to their inability to provide first aid and transport him for treatment to Kamal Adwan Hospital, which is only 700 meters away. The agony is compounded by the fact that his body is still in front of his family and loved ones due to their inability to bury him in the cemetery.

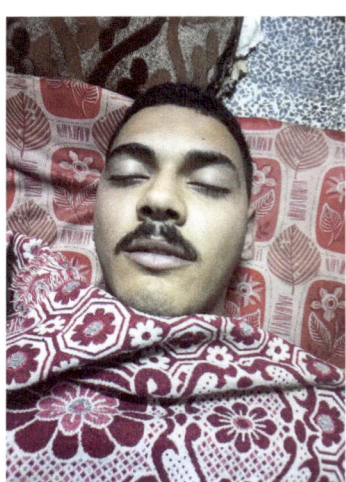

Innocence Lost: The Tragic Tale of Huda and Her Unborn Daughter

My heart aches to share the tragic story of my cousin Huda Salem, who was seriously injured during the savage bombardment of the Al-Zeitoun School in northern Gaza by the occupation, which led to the death of more than 50 martyrs. Huda was unjustly martyred less than a year after her marriage. She was eight months pregnant with her first daughter, dreaming of living under her and her father's love. Huda passed away miraculously after giving birth to her fetus, as doctors performed a difficult cesarean section operation amidst the lack of resources and medical supplies. This is the new story of pain that the child will bear, after being separated from her mother without any fault on her part. Her only fault is being a Palestinian who wants to live in peace on her land.

When she grows up, her innocent heart will burn with inquiries.

Did I come into this world without a mother?

Where was the one who was supposed to hold me?

Did my mother martyr herself to save me from certain death?

Why did the occupation take my mother from me?

My only wish is for my mother to style my hair when I go to kindergarten after she prepares my breakfast sandwich!

Mahmoud: A Life of Sacrifice, Strength, and Faith

Mahmoud graduated from the College of Business Administration and Finance just days before the war, with honors. Mahmoud, with a face full of life and eyes filled with passion and determination for those who knew him, was the epitome of a diligent and ambitious young man. He loved business administration and excelled in his studies, as well as in his practical thinking and application. He began working on establishing his own project before graduation and was ready to launch it if not for the onset of the war.

Light-hearted and possessing a playful and humorous spirit, he dealt with matters with simplicity despite bearing full responsibility. He brought a cheerful atmosphere to everyone around him, especially to his mother, sisters, and the children of the household. He was close to everyone's heart and was a generous and noble servant, always willing to share knowledge and help both relatives and strangers.

He concluded his days striving to please his parents even before his martyrdom. He used to walk tens of kilometers on foot to get medicine and painkillers for his father who was suffering from cancer. His father passed away two days before his martyrdom due to being prevented from traveling to continue his treatment, on December 28, 2023.

Everyone knew Mahmoud for his sharp intellect and noble character. He lived valiantly, never satisfied with the worldly life.

My friends and I were sitting around the lunch table, discussing life's challenges and the hardships faced by our people in Gaza. Each shared the struggles of their families. Suddenly, our close friend received a call from Gaza. As he spoke on the phone, standing at a distance, we strained to catch his words, knowing these types of calls often carry sorrowful news.

There was a heaviness in his tone, but amidst the conversation, we caught the words "Praise be to Allah" We exchanged concerned glances, fearing the worst. Just two days prior, he received news that his father had passed away due to an illness he couldn't seek treatment for.

The fear lingered as we anticipated the news of his brother's fate. But our friend's reaction was unexpectedly poignant. "Praise be to God, who has chosen among us the martyrs," he uttered, acknowledging that this was a wish his brother had held dear.

The hardest task lay ahead – how to break this heart-wrenching news to his mother. After many attempts, He finally got through to her. I stood by, silently in my mind pleading, "Please, don't tell her," while our friend, with tremendous strength, conveyed the devastating news. "Mother, I know that you are strong. Praise be to Allah who chose the martyrs among us, and Mahmoud is now among them."

Her response was both heartbreaking and inspiring. "Praise be to our Allah, under all circumstances. Today, Mahmoud is a groom in Paradise," then she began to ululate and ask those around her to do so.

.In the face of unimaginable loss, their unwavering faith and strength shone through, leaving us in awe of their resilience and devotion.

Victims of Hope: Youssef Ghubn

In the depths of northern Gaza, where the cries of hungry children rise above the din of battle, lived Youssef Ghubn, a 55-year-old man, a loyal and brave neighbor. His eyes carried an indescribable sadness, a sadness for a lost past and a tortured present, yet in his heart beat a pulse of hope and generosity.

Youssef lived in a modest little house just 100 meters away from ours. Our neighbor, who was once a close friend in school, told me, "Youssef was incredibly brilliant and one of the best students. He achieved a high score in the high school exams, then he asked his family to travel to Germany to study medicine, but due to the family's economic situation, he couldn't travel and became a farmer." He was a man of his word, loved by people, always ready to offer them goodness whenever he could. Youssef took care of his blind mother and his sick son.

Amidst this war, like many others, Youssef sought refuge in places where there is no safety because no one is spared from the bombing. In the first few weeks, the northern Gaza Strip exhausted its stock of food from its homes and stores, and residents resorted to searching in abandoned or unoccupied houses for canned goods or frozen items. Some residents recount how they were forced to remove the doors of abandoned shops in search of something to satisfy their hunger and feed their families, after their food supplies ran out.

The specter of famine began to appear on the remaining inhabitants of northern Gaza, with Israel's insistence on preventing the entry of any food aid, amidst waves of violent aerial bombardment and fierce ground confrontations with the resistance. In the southern and central areas of Gaza, living conditions remained relatively better than in the north, with limited numbers of aid trucks entering. However, the influx of hundreds of thousands of displaced people from the north of the Strip put pressure on the stock of food in these areas and increased the need for larger quantities of humanitarian aid, which remained unchanged.

The residents of northern Gaza resorted to the arduous search for any food they could consume, and the situation reached the point where they ground animal feed and poultry feed for consumption, and searched the agricultural lands for any vegetation that could sustain them.

Amidst Israel's tightening grip on the entry of aid via land routes, countries attempted to deliver aid by air and sea. However, the humiliating aerial drops, as people called them, diminished the value of the aid, and dropping a trivial symbolic amount of aid without a safe distribution plan would not help them.

In the hell of waiting, where hope and despair wrestle on the shores of the sea, Youssef's story was painted in the colors of suffering and sacrifice, amidst this constant struggle between life and death, in a world dominated by the colors of occupation and oppression.

The atmosphere was charged with loss and pain, and every day witnessed long moments of arduous waiting, as people gathered on the shores of the sea, searching for drops of mercy falling from the sky to feed their hunger and elevate their hope.

Youssef, the brave man who did not surrender to the tyranny of circumstances, defied the cold currents to obtain the necessary food for his family. He crossed the lines of danger without hesitation, ready to pay any price for survival.

But, in a silent and crushing moment, as this aid fell into the sea, he went to dive into the depths of the sea in search of a few bites to satisfy their hunger. The fierce winds came carrying with them the painful testimony.

His cold body fell beneath the waves, suffocating his hope for survival, and rising as a martyr.

In this bitter moment, sorrow and grief swept through the hearts of the people, knowing that Youssef was not the only one who decided to risk his life for a cause bigger than himself, the cause of survival and dignity.

In this land besieged by famine and blockade, where the occupation controls every aspect of life, the people continue to struggle for survival, day after day, with a strength and determination that never wavers, and through stories of sacrifice and redemption, they continue to weave a legend of unending resilience, under the shadows of oppression and injustice, showing the world that truth and dignity will not be broken, and that life continues despite all the hardships and challenges.

Echoes of the Islamic University: From Magnificence to Ruin

In the heart of Gaza city, the towering buildings of the Islamic University rise as magnificent symbols of knowledge and progress. Its towers and landmarks blend beautifully with the surrounding nature, as tall trees and seasonal flowers harmonize with its white walls, creating an unmatched allure.

Upon entering its gates, the university transforms into a world filled with life and activity. The academic spirit seamlessly merges with the vitality of movement, as the sound of students' footsteps fills the corridors and echoes with their laughter and scholarly discussions.

In the grand conference hall, the grandeur of knowledge and research is evident, as minds converge on one platform to explore the depths of knowledge and exchange groundbreaking ideas. The horizon expands to welcome the thoughts of scholars and researchers, providing attendees with an exhilarating and enriching experience that stimulates the mind and fosters creativity.

And in graduation ceremonies, students shine with pride and exuberance for their achievements. The hall is filled with joy and happiness, and smiles adorn the faces of graduates and their families, in moments where pride in accomplishment merges with hope for a bright future.

In the depths of the silent night, and under a sky shrouded in darkness, the Islamic University hides like a beautiful bird in its nest. It was the beacon of light in a sea of ignorance, and the lamp of knowledge in a time of darkness. It was a refuge for aspiring students, and a center for research and education.

However, the days of war came, those days filled with bloodshed and destruction, those days when peace evaporated like mist before the fire of conflicts. The Islamic University was subjected to violent attacks, and nothing remained but rubble and memories.

In the corners of the ruins, silence creeps like deep sorrow, and every piece of stone feels the pain of loss and defeat. Memories of past days intertwine with scenes of destruction, as echoes of laughter and scholarly discussions dance with the fragments of burnt buildings and shattered dreams.

And as mournful researchers gather around the rubble, they recall in their memory their wise teachers and dear colleagues, who were lost in the turmoil of war. They struggle with pain and sorrow, but they hold onto the spark of hope in their hearts, and pledge to build a new future on the ashes of the past.

And thus, despite its horrific destruction, the Islamic University remains alive in the memory of all who knew and loved it. For buildings may fall and stones may crumble, but knowledge will not die, and the educational spirit will not vanish, for it lives among generations like a beacon that continues to shine even in the depths of darkness.

In Gaza, everything now exists solely as memories.

March 5th, 2015, a day of unparalleled significance in my life and a pinnacle for anyone who sacrificed sleep and toil. It marked my university graduation, a day where I gathered all my loved ones to share in my joy. The sheer elation of my parents, who gave their all to see me through, remains etched in my mind. I recall renting a camera to seize every moment of that day. It symbolized the culmination of four years of hard work and late nights. I remember every detail of the graduation hall, the tears and cheers of family and friends, their collective support lifting me as if it were a wedding day. I also remember walking through the university grounds, a mother asking for a photo with her son, hoping he would follow a similar path.

The once-celebrated hall, witness to the ascent of countless scholars, doctors, engineers, teachers, and more, now lies in ruins, a casualty of brutal Israeli attacks.

"In Gaza, everything now exists solely as memories."

6. Hope Amidst Hardship

Spirit of Resilience: Gaza Between Its Sands and Sea

In a confined space representing the most densely populated area in the world, the people of Gaza live on the land of the Gaza Strip, which troubles the unjust world. As you walk through the streets of Gaza, traversing from east to west and from north to south, you find no respite except in the Mediterranean Sea, which occupies a position of hope for the Gazans. Despite their participation in the siege imposed upon them by political, military, and economic systems worldwide, this does not deter them from continuing their project of liberation from the forces of oppression and tyranny.

While wandering the streets, everything appears besieged except for three things: "the salty sea, the Gazan intellect, and the generous Palestinian spirit." Thus, if you were to liken the Gaza Strip to something, it would be akin to living on a semi-island with all its borders closed except for the sea. However, the occupiers spare no effort in placing maritime barriers and naval obstacles to hinder the work of the Palestinian fishermen seeking their livelihood amidst the depths of the sea, whose full details only its Creator knows.

Amidst the life of war in Gaza, love cannot be stripped from their lives. Just as pain exists, so does hope, emerging from the wheat fields, the sands of the beach, and the colorful azure sky of the turbulent blue sea at times and the tranquil sea at others. The Gazan is sometimes deluded into believing that he carries all hope, but it is a hope with the taste of salty water, as the sea embodies the miracles of its Creator, Almighty and Exalted.

In the midst of the war on Gaza, and as the means for a decent life, considered the most basic human rights, are cut off, and amidst the displacement of over a million and a half Palestinians from the areas of Gaza City and its north to the southern regions of the Gaza Strip, particularly Rafah, and the interruption of clean drinking water, the occupation did not suffice with that. It also prevented Palestinians from their right to bathe, a right considered fundamental for every human being, even if they were prisoners. Thus, the Palestinian is forced to go to the sea to take a dose of hope amidst all the pains he lives and swallows moment by moment. This becomes a form of challenge for the Palestinian against the occupier of his land for more than seven decades.

Among the rubble of stones and the pain of parting from loved ones, the hope emerges vividly from the azure of the sea despite its salinity, the crashing of its waves, the fierceness of its winds, the yellowness of its sands, and the goldenness of its sun that rises anew every day to instill hope in the hearts of the Palestinians amidst the rubble of pain, waterfalls of blood, and mountains of debris.

And so, the people of Gaza continue to write the story of resilience and hope on pages tainted with the blood of martyrs and the tears of orphans. They resist with all the strength they possess, not only to preserve their existence but also to prove to the world that life is worth the suffering and fighting. They cherish it despite its harshness and build bridges of hope across the seas of darkness.

Beneath the Rubble

In the northern Gaza Strip, where beautiful white houses blend with narrow alleys and bustling streets, the specter of war loomed large. When Israel began its latest military campaign, residents of the northern area were asked to evacuate to southern areas for protection from the intense bombardment that was intensifying.

The decisions were tough, and fears were high. While some chose to leave, seeking refuge in what was believed to be safer areas as claimed by the occupation, others decided to stay in their homes. They refused the idea of leaving their properties and land, despite the looming threat of death and destruction surrounding them. "Death in our homes is

better than leaving them," was a phrase echoed on their tongues, expressing their attachment to their rights and identity, and their determination to stay in their land despite all hardships and risks.

At the same time, some ventured to the southern region of the Strip in an attempt to avoid the danger of bombing and death. And although they left their homes, they did not abandon hope of returning. They patiently awaited the day they could return to their homes.

Despite the massive destruction witnessed in the northern Gaza Strip, some of the people who were forced to evacuate to southern areas did not succumb to the harsh conditions and increasing risks. Instead, they expressed their strong determination to return to their destroyed homes despite all the risks.

In their simple attempts to return to the northern area, they faced extremely difficult obstacles, with roads surrounded by Israeli tanks and snipers positioned on rooftops, and soldiers armed with various weapons. Yet even amid this horrific scene, they did not waver in their decision to return.

تصوير: هاني الشاعر

Some tried to cross the barriers silently and cautiously, in an attempt to avoid detection by the soldiers, but others chose not to settle for cautious steps, opting instead for direct confrontation, in a clear challenge to the occupying forces.

In these harsh confrontations, some of these brave individuals were martyred, leaving behind traces of courage and unwavering determination. Their sacrifices remain a symbol of resilience and determination in the face of cruelty and injustice, and a reminder that hope and faith in justice can never be defeated even in the toughest of circumstances.

And so, amidst those who stay and those who leave, and with each passing day and with every exploding shell, the yearning for home grows. Some continue to endure in their destroyed homes, repairing what can be repaired, and living in the shadows of fear and constant threats. And others, who were forced to evacuate, eagerly await the moment they can return, to rebuild their lives and reclaim their lost identity in northern Gaza, amidst memories of the past and hope for a brighter future.

Journeying Through Darkness Towards Hope

In the depths of the pitch-black night, under a canopy of clouds heavy with sorrow and death, Gaza was living through unforgettable moments of misery and despair. Its streets had turned into corridors of pain, and its homes into tombs for buried dreams.

Amidst the ongoing war and the worsening famine that had struck northern Gaza, people embarked on a desperate and painful journey towards hope and survival. The aid dropped from the sky by the influential nations represented the last moment of hope, and thus the people were ready to risk it all for these scattered hopes in the sky.

Hunger filled their souls, and loss permeated their bones, yet despite this, the love for life and resilience pushed them forward on this perilous journey. They knew that the road to safety was not easy, and danger lurked at every corner, but despair had not yet consumed them.

The aid falling from the sky represented their last meal, the morsel that could grant them another day in this dark world. Humanitarian food and medical supplies were scattered from the sky like dewdrops in a barren desert.

And so, people marched forth with courage and determination to face the challenges and risks, carrying in their hearts the longing for life and the desire to build a better future for their families and children. Every drop of water and every bag of flour falling from the sky represented a new lease on life, a fresh opportunity for survival and resilience.

Despite the intense need and suffering, people continued to strive for those hopes scattered in the sky, confident that the light would come someday, and that life would sprout again in the land of hope.

With every drop of blood shed, the spirit of resistance and resilience grew stronger, and with every martyr who fell, the will to survive and cling to life increased. In the end, through their sacrifices and solidarity, they managed to reach the port of safety, carrying with them the stories of the martyrs and the dreams of the survivors, and in their hands, the bag of flour that had become a symbol of resilience and hope.

Their journey was not just a quest for aid, but a journey into the depths of humanity, where they surged forward with strength towards life and hope despite all odds and trials.

Resilience Under the Sky

In the depths of darkness and under the canopy of clouds laden with blackness, people lived in their humble tents amidst the sounds of shells and bombs echoing on the horizon. Their lives were filled with suffering and challenges, yet they continued to confront the fierce Israeli war with courage and determination.

Amidst the violent airstrikes targeting their homes in northern Gaza, they were forced to flee to the south in search of a safe haven. And so, they found themselves living in modest tents, offering them little protection from the biting cold of the night and the scorching heat of the day.

The tents became a makeshift community for them, where they shared each other's pain and hope. Women worked tirelessly to prepare food over intermittent fires, while men sought to secure basic resources and protect their families from any potential danger.

Every morning, children woke up to the sound of bombs echoing in the distance, starting their day by gathering the scattered remnants of life around the tent. Despite the harsh conditions, the innocence of their children and their innocent smiles illuminated their hearts and gave them the strength to move forward.

The nights passed slowly, laden with fear and anxiety, as people surrendered to the sounds of shelling and explosions, wondering if tomorrow would bring light or if darkness would continue to engulf them.

But even in the deepest darkness, they did not lose hope. Prayers rose to the sky, and supplications transcended the boundaries between hope and despair, believing that God would protect them and grant them victory in the end.

As the days and nights passed, they began to build a new community in these tents, defying war and adversity, united in resilience and solidarity. The tents were not just a temporary shelter, but a symbol of their strength and determination, and a home for hope and challenge.

And so, amidst the folds of the simple tents, people continue with their daily lives, facing challenges and struggling for their survival, awaiting the day when the sun of peace and security will rise over Gaza, and life returns to its normalcy after the journey of wars and suffering comes to an end.

One woman, amidst the ruins of her demolished home, says as she tries to gather what remains of her house, "By God, even if the whole world gathers against Gaza, Gaza will prevail. Jerusalem's dowry is precious, and Palestine's dowry is precious." Another woman, standing atop the ashes of her destroyed home, declares, "No matter how much the occupation bombs, no matter what it does to the people of Gaza, no matter how long or short the time, we will reclaim and return to our land. The occupation will eventually disappear, no matter how long it takes. Palestine is our land, and we will not abandon it. No one will relinquish their rights. Let every occupier return to their homeland. We are steadfast and proud, like the proud mountains of Palestine."

Acknowledgements

To everyone who contributed to the completion of this book, I extend my deepest gratitude and appreciation. To those who supported me morally, and to everyone who entrusted me with their photographs, allowing me to document the reality of life in Gaza, your contributions were more than just acts of support; they were a living testament to the resilience of the Palestinian spirit that refuses to break.

I am especially grateful to my family and friends, who stood by my side throughout this literary journey, offering unwavering encouragement and belief in the value of this work. To my people, who, despite pain and siege, remain a beacon of awareness and an unyielding voice of truth.

To all of you, I say with love and gratitude: you are the heart of this book, and without you, it would not have been complete.

About the Author

Shadi Salem is a Palestinian writer and researcher with a Master's degree in Applied Linguistics from the Islamic University of Gaza. He is the co-founder of the Edward Said Library in Gaza, which has become a cultural platform that promotes awareness and knowledge. He also manages a Malaysian cultural center in Gaza and has participated in international cultural programs aimed at fostering dialogue and cultural exchange. Through his writings and initiatives, he strives to amplify Gaza's voice and shed light on the reality of his people, their struggles, resilience, and aspirations.